The

Village

Clock

. . . .

Mahmood writes with a quiet elegance that seems to bring the past closer still, as if his carefully chosen syllables enunciate a world in which each noise still has a significance, not yet swallowed up in the indecipherable clamour so familiar today. His book is a treasure.

—Aram Saroyan (poet, novelist, biographer)
Complete Minimal Poems

The

Village

Clock

a

collection

of folk

tales

Arshud Mahmood

Artwork by AliA

Edited by Martha Fuller
Layout and design by Sharon E Rawlins
Artwork by AliA

INDUS WEST
induswest22@gmail.com
Tustin, California

First Edition 1999
Second Edition 2023

ISBN (Print) #979-8-9870810-2-0
ISBN (eBook) #979-8-9870810-3-7

Printed in the United States of America

For Soraya, my granddaughter

With best wishes for her success and happiness

CONTENTS

Prologue

. . . .

As a child, I learned these stories from my grandmother and over the years they became a hazy memory. As an adult, I heard them again from my father. His re-telling brought them alive for me and I was able to produce this collection.

Auntie Ji

*A*untie *Ji* had gotten lost again. She managed to do this almost every time she came to visit. I just tried another short cut, she explained later. This is such a maze of alleys around here. When are you going to get some street signs?

She had ended up in the wrong alley this time and decided to rest at an acquaintance's house. No one complained, for she always brought presents for the kids; not useful presents like sweaters or school supplies, but things kids really liked: toys and *mithai*—their favorite sweetmeats. She was also a great storyteller.

Our outer gate was six feet high, wide enough for a horse carriage, and made of sturdy cast-iron with ornate spikes. It opened into a courtyard that was surrounded by four red-brick row houses that comprised our family compound. When Auntie Ji entered the family compound from the outer gate, with an armful of goodies, she gave out her usual yell.

Children, your villager Auntie has arrived!

Each house in our compound had an open front veranda, and the children poured out from the verandas to greet her with joyful shouts.

Auntie Ji is here; Auntie Ji is here.

She was soon surrounded by a brood, hugging her, and helping to unload her armload of packages filled with village sweetmeats and handcrafted wooden toys. The children never counted how many days she stayed, and apparently, she didn't either. By the third or fourth week, a message would arrive from her family. The crop is ready. We are going to start harvesting next week.

Let them harvest it; they can manage without me, she would say. No one can eat a grain that has my name on it, my share will still be there when I get back.

Fatalist doesn't quite describe her. She always seemed to inhabit a different dimension, perhaps a skewed one. By evening she had washed and changed into clean white clothes: a fine cotton *Kameez* (a long, dress-like shirt), coarse cotton *Shalwar* (loose, baggy pants tied with a cummerbund) and a muslin *Dupatta* (a

6

large veil-like cloth loosely placed over head and shoulders). With her all-white clothing in the dimly lit courtyard, she had the look of an apparition.

You look like an angel, elder Uncle Noor commented, and everyone laughed.

Dinner was prepared in the courtyard kitchen and eaten while sitting on low stools made of hemp. It was mid-summer, and the kids were going to be sleeping in the open courtyard on cots laid out in rows. The youngsters looked forward to bedtime.

As soon as dinner was over, a chorus went up, Tell us a story, Auntie Ji.

· · · · · · · · ·

Auntie Ji, a lively story teller, would always open a window to the past with her simple but intriguing tales of family, history, and incidents from village life.

Once upon a time. . .

The Village Clock

*A*untie *Ji* settled in and said to one of the young girls—Your grandfather, Raheem, was the eldest in his family. He excelled in school as a child and was encouraged to continue to high school. There was no high school in the village where they lived, so he rode a bike nine miles each way to the city, most of it along a macadam track. He matriculated in 1895 with distinction from high school, applied for admission to college and was accepted. He took the acceptance papers to his father.

I want to go to college, he said, but I will have to do a lot of homework and study very hard. I want to move to the city.

Son, his father said, we have no money to send you to live in the city.

So, grandfather dropped the idea of going to college and decided to look for employment in the city. He had an older cousin, Amin, who was working as an English-language clerk in the Irrigation Department. He rode his bike to the city and found the cousin in his office.

Brother, he said, I need to obtain employ-ment. Can you help me? Amin helped him find a clerical job in the same department.

His office was in a musty old brick building, where rows of clerks sat in a large room. Heavy wooden desks and chairs had been built to last, but were not very comfortable to work in. The pace of work in the office was slow as molasses. Each desk had stacks of Manila files tied with sturdy woven cotton straps. Peons stood around and when asked, moved the files from one desk to the next. The clerks sat back in their chairs, chatted with each other, took breaks for drink-ing tea, smoking, and reading newspapers. Occasionally they scribbled some notes in the bulging files. These clerks proved what people said of the British Empire. The Empire had built public schools to train future clerks to sit still for long periods. As an office clerk, Grandpa Raheem had to sit in a chair all day and work at a desk.

Raheem grew up on the farm and was used to a strenuous outdoor life. He was a handsome and muscular young man. At harvest time he could pick up two sacks of wheat, one under

11

each arm, and climb up a bamboo ladder to the grain storage shed on the roof. After two months of office work, he couldn't take it any longer and went to his cousin.

Brother Amin, he said, I cannot sit in a chair all day. I need a job that requires walking about. If I sit in a chair all day, my life will be over in a few years.

Amin also came from the farm and understood the feeling of confinement, but he had adapted himself to the life in an office for good reasons.

As an English language clerk, you have double the salary of a native language clerk, and greater access to the supervisor, he said. After twenty years or so, you could even become a supervisor.

But your grandfather was not impressed. He asked his cousin if any other kind of a job was available. The cousin made some inquiries, and after a few days informed Grandpa Raheem.

The only other job available is in the irrigation department as a canal inspector, Amin said. It requires travel along the canals and inspection of water outlets. You will have to assign irrigation water to the farmers.

That sounds perfect, Grandpa Raheem said. This way I'll always be close to the flowing water and green fields. He knew there were good tracks along all the canal banks, and he could travel on his bicycle.

Hear me out first, Amin said. Your salary as a canal inspector will be only one half of what you make as an office clerk. Think about that.

Grandpa Raheem thought for a couple of days and then accepted the position. Now he could visit the villages, breathe clean fresh air, and get out of the city where he felt shut in. Over the next several years he visited many villages and spent time close to the village life.

During one of his visits, he saw a peculiar and amusing incident that took place in a small village. The farmers in the village shared the irrigation water from a canal about two miles away. Water was controlled at a small outlet with a gate that opened into a water supply ditch leading to the fields. Each farmer diverted the water to his fields for a fixed number of hours.

13

They estimated the watering time by looking at the position of the sun during the day, and the moon or stars during the night.

The older, more experienced farmers could estimate watering time precisely, but some of the younger ones made errors. Instead of patiently learning how to tell time from the sun, moon, and stars, they wanted a change of procedure.

We think the village should purchase a clock, one of the younger villagers proposed to the village elders one day. Although the elders had their doubts about this change, they agreed to buy a clock.

Contributions were taken from the families who owned farmland around the village. One of the villagers traveled to the city and purchased a large wall clock for twenty rupees. The clock was put in a prominent position in the village community hall, and they began using it to measure watering time.

The clock had a large white dial and numbers and hands that could be seen very clearly. The young men immediately took to it, though some of the older farmers needed help in the beginning. Soon the clock became the pride of the village; when kinsfolk from neighboring villages came to visit, the elders made a point of showing off the clock as an example of progress.

We use this clock to reckon watering time, an elder would explain. It is as reliable as the sun, and now even the young boys can be precise in irrigating the fields. The farmers felt they had entered the modern age.

The clock needed winding once a week. The village watchman was assigned this task, and he performed it dutifully, until the annual Harvest Festival arrived. Amidst all the activities and parties, the watchman forgot to wind the clock. That night an older villager who was waiting for his turn to water his fields came to check the clock. Something was wrong; he looked at the position of the moon, and the clock was too slow. He was sure it was time for his watering cycle and the clock was wrong. This damned thing is not working correctly, he murmured to himself. He opened the clock, moved the hands forward by an hour and walked out to divert the water to his own fields.

As the farmer was leaving, he saw the watchman and told him, Your time contraption is not working. The watchman remembered he had forgotten his weekly assignment, went in and wound the clock. Early the next morning, another farmer saw the sun coming up, looked at the clock and could see that it was too fast. He moved the clock hands back by a couple of hours to extend the watering time to his own farm.

I forgot to wind up the clock yesterday, the watchman mentioned to another farmer later that day. It has now been corrected.

The following day this farmer adjusted the clock. By the end of the month the clock's hands were being moved back and forth two, three, sometimes four times a week to calibrate to the position of the sun, the moon, the length of the shadows, or anything else. One night a farmer caught another one tampering with the clock.

What do you think you are doing? the farmer asked.

Didn't you see the full moon rise almost an hour ago? It is my turn to water the fields. This clock is obviously wrong. I am going to correct it so I can divert the water.

No, you are not, because that will shorten my watering cycle. I started watering by this clock, and I am going to end my cycle by this clock. I don't care about the moon.

Their argument became louder and more colorful. One of them commented on the other farmer's ancestry in impolite language. The other replied in kind, mentioning all the missing links in the lyrical Punjabi language. Blows were exchanged, and the farmer who had been caught tampering with the clock returned home with a bloody nose and a torn shirt. Male members of his extended family gathered early in the morning, and about a dozen of them marched towards the other farmer's house. Two were carrying their swords, and two brought shotguns. Halfway to the other farmhouse they were met by their opponents. They also had brought a couple of swords, one rifle and two axes. It was a matter of family honor, and a bloody family feud was about to begin. Fortunately, other nearby families intervened,

17

and the dispute was presented to the hurriedly assembled village elders.

I am a simple, honest man, the first farmer said solemnly. I don't want to cheat anyone, but I will not give up what is my right. You know how delicate the cotton seedlings are; my fields need water, and I was only trying to start my watering period at the appropriate time. The clock is obviously wrong.

My fields also need water. The other farmer was equally steadfast. The mustard plants have just sprouted, and if they become stunted, the ripened seeds will not have even half the yield. I began my irrigation period by the clock, and I must complete it the same way. The moon is pretty to watch, but it is not precise for time-keeping. We must follow the clock or else the whole water allotment system becomes a joke.

After listening to the two farmers, the elders began questioning other witnesses and neighbors. It became apparent that clock tampering was quite widespread. Several farmers admitted to having adjusted the clock, and they felt insulted that their judgement and skill in estimating the passage of time was being compared with that of a clock that stopped when it was not wound. They believed they were in the right and merely correcting errors made by the clock.

The feud between the two families was all but forgotten, while the whole community grew more and more upset about the clock's performance. The elders faced a dilemma. All the witnesses were reliable, honorable men, and solid members of the community. The elders could not take sides and satisfy everyone. After some deliberation one of the elders stood up to announce their decision.

There were no arguments about irrigation water in the community before the clock arrived, the elder said. We can find no fault with the individuals who were trying to correct errors made by the clock. We have reached our decisions: the clock has caused discord in our community, and it must be punished.

It was at this point that Grandpa Raheem approached the village. He always dressed well with a fancy vest and tall turban. He carried his government-stamped leather valise tied on the bicycle carrier behind him and was easily recognizable as a government official. He had been riding the bicycle along the track on the canal bank, admiring the newly sown fields. The canal bank was raised above the adjacent ground, and he got a clear view of the village from across the fields. He could see the earthen adobe houses and as he got close, he noticed that many villagers were gathered outside the community hall.

As he approached the gathering, the proceedings were halted and the villagers parted to allow him through.

What is the matter? he asked one of villagers. What has happened?

The villager pointed to the center of the gathering where a large clock was lying on the ground and two young men with axes were ready to take swings. They were waiting for the elder's signal to execute the clock publicly, as it was held responsible for their discord. The canal inspector's arrival interrupted the proceedings, some of the elders knew him and exchanged greetings. One of the elders told him about the clock that had brought disunity to the village.

Don't destroy the clock, Grandpa Raheem said to the elder. I'll buy it from you.

A couple of elders were against it, as a sale would violate the sentence they had pronounced against the clock. After some debate, they agreed to sell the clock to Grandpa Raheem, on the condition he immediately carry it out of the village.

He had three rupees in his pocket that he offered to them. They accepted the money; he rode out of the village with the clock tied on the carrier behind him and brought it home. It was an Ansonia clock, made in the USA, and it worked well in our house until the second Great War.

As Auntie finished the story, some of the younger children were beginning to doze off. The next morning two of the older boys were caught trying to adjust the large family clock to delay their departure to school.

The Other Woman

The next day was a school holiday. The kids slept till late, and then went to the playground. During the early evening some distant relatives were arriving, and dinner was delayed while some of the adults went to the train station to pick them up. The kids didn't mind, as it gave them extra time for games in the courtyard. However, when the late dinner was over, the kids were too tired to stay up, and went to bed.

After dinner several women gathered to chat and get to know the visiting relatives. The men had gone out for smoking and to complete their business dealings. The conversation in the women's gathering had turned to stories of married life. One of the visiting ladies, who looked very distinguished, had been quiet as other women traded the details about their husbands, marriages, and personal lives, while making sure no young girls were within earshot. Finally, Auntie Ji asked this lady, Sister Sohni, why don't you tell us a story from your life. After some hesitation, Sohni began.

I can still remember the early years of our marriage. He was not the romantic hero of love stories I had dreamed my husband would be, but he was kind, and gentle and caring.

How is my Sohni? He would look for me as soon as he walked into the house, and hand me a package with some small personal gift—an article of makeup or my favorite snack—and pat me gently. My name means pretty woman, and he said it in a way that made me blush. If his aunt or uncle were not around, the pat would linger into a caress.

After, I would catch him up on the day's activities. The scribe brought two letters. Your cousin stopped by and said the winter wheat should be ready by next week, so don't go out of town. And the stable boy said one of the horses does not look too good. I was always full of news for him, wanted to talk, but it was not romantic conversation. My love and passion for him was rarely expressed in words.

It was different at night. Although he is from a small village like me, he studied at a school in the city, and could both read and write English. He had picked up some city-folk ways. These included inhibitions I had not observed in the village boys. It must be true that schooling makes you overly cautions.

I come from a little village where men, women, boys and girls all worked side by side. Some of the heavier farm chores like plowing were reserved for men, but everyone worked. The women did not sit around merely watching the kids, as I saw happen during my one visit to the city. I had never felt any inhibition in approaching men—I *had* to talk to them to get all the tasks completed.

We continued a passionate life for many years. We had no children, but he didn't seem to mind. Suddenly he began to turn cool toward me. At first I couldn't figure out why. Then one night I overheard his aunt talking to him in hushed tones.

For sixteen years you have been married to her, and she has not borne you a child.

How long are you going to tolerate this behavior?

It is not her fault, Auntie. And Sohni has been a good wife.

How is our family name going to be carried on. I say discard her and marry again.

I shrank back from behind the door, went to the bedroom and collapsed on my bed. Discard me? Was he planning to divorce me? What was going to happen to me? My mind was paralyzed. Divorce or separation was social death.

In this village community I was never again going to be eligible for marriage; everyone would know why I had been discarded. I could move back to my village and live with my parents, but it would be a servant's life, mere existence. There would never be another proposal and I would never have a home I could call my own.

For the following month, the thought of it all didn't leave my mind. I was worried. I knew I had to do something, or it would be all over. I had to find out his thoughts and get control of the situation. At first it felt repulsive, even strange, but the more I thought, the more it seemed the only way out.

I am going to find a second wife for him, I declared to Sara, my girlfriend since childhood and my confidante.

A wife? She seemed perplexed.

Yes, a wife. It is legal. And in a situation like this it would be quite proper. I know him, Sara. He wants a child, and he is under tremendous family pressure.

Right here, right in your own house; how can you think of him going to bed with another woman? Sara had always been emotional.

Either I can arrange for it, and keep control of the situation, or that witch aunt of his is going to do it, I said. But it made no impression on her.

How can you even think of sharing your husband with anyone?

I can either share him, or totally lose him. I am not going to let foolish prudery stand in the way. I know what people are going to say, but I don't care.

But how can you bear the thought of another woman in his bed? Sara was having difficulty separating romance from procreation.

I grew up on the farm. We had livestock. I know how breeding takes place. I am going to manage this. I will select the girl.

I had been able to interpret his thoughts many times in the past, and I trusted my intuition. He wanted someone to arrange it and get rid of me in the process.

I began making enquiries about the eligible young women in our village and expanded my search to a couple of neighboring villages. At first it was difficult for me, but I had to put my emotions aside. Some people thought I was looking for a mate for my brother who lived in the city. I remained noncommittal and started to narrow down my choices. It had to be a young girl who would not challenge my authority in the household. She should not be from a large or very rich family so her parents would not have to contend with too much advice from family members. I did not want a peasant girl, but she had to be sturdy and reasonably attractive.

Girls in a small village are observed through-out their childhood and puberty by neighbors and extended families. I learned details from families who had been scouting for suitable mates for their sons. Soon I had selected a girl. She was a little over sixteen years old, tall, sturdy and pretty without being too delicate. She was pleasant company and laughed easily. Her family owned land, but they were not rich or overly educated and had a reputation as solid community members. After visiting her house a few times, I believed the girl and I could get along.

The girl's parents were apprehensive about the potential conflict between two wives sharing one husband. I assured them that it was my idea. I would not let envy create problems. This was being done for my family honor and to carry the family name forward. My husband owned land, came from a good family, and was schooled in the city. They knew they were not going to receive another proposal like this. Their daughter was going to live comfortably with a husband who made a good living. They just had to trust me to be fair. I convinced them. I don't know if I convinced myself.

The preparations for the wedding reminded me more of my doll-playing days than my own wedding. Once or twice, I teased him, What do you think of this red dress for your new bride?

He seemed both embarrassed and pleased. Clothes and jewelry took about three months to prepare. Sara, I said to my girlfriend, let us go to the jeweler.

Sohni, you are disgusting, how can you remain so calm?

I had insisted that the wedding necklace be made by one of the jewelers in the city—I did not trust the goldsmith in the village, not after the way he had ruined my jewelry. I owned a set of heavy gold bangles made by the village goldsmith and never liked it. I decided to have it melted down and recast into earrings and a choker for the girl by a city jeweler. In addition, there would be a new gold necklace, bangles and rings. In proper Punjabi fashion, all jewelry had to be solid 24 carat gold. Anything less would dishonor the girl's family. All the busy work and

31

preparations helped me keep my mind off the emotional impact of the approaching event.

She looked so young and innocent on the wedding day. The wedding night was very rough on me. Fortunately, much of the time I was kept busy feeding and looking after all the relatives that had come to attend the wedding from out of town.

So what are you thinking, Sohni? Sara asked, late on the wedding night after the bride and groom had retired for the evening.

Sara, he has not made love to me in two years. I was going to lose him anyway. This way this is still my home. I think I was finally beginning to convince her, even though my own confidence was withering.

I had overheard a guest saying, Look, how saintly Sohni looks. She is really selfless. I must have begun projecting a very unemotional facade. Indeed, my self-control was being taken for my piety. I was not yet ready for sainthood but kept my cool.

Days passed and he seemed pleased with her. She treated me with respect and asked my permission before doing almost anything in the house. I kept control of the money and other matters pertaining to running the household and allowed her to concentrate on her duties. I told her about his preferences, likes and dislikes. I allowed her to do little tasks that I knew would please him. I came to like her, and she was pleasant company by the second year, which is when she became pregnant.

She showed almost immediately, and it was a source of pride for him in the extended family. He would break into a smile without any reason. As pregnancy advanced, he began showing an interest in me. I wasn't sure whether he was being appreciative for all I had done, or his feelings had reawakened. I did not care, and it was nice to be close to him again.

The childbirth was normal. It was a healthy boy. I was determined to remain aloof and not become emotionally involved with the child. I did not have a little baby to take care of, so my husband slept in my room almost every night.

I have to go to work early, and the boy hardly sleeps at night, he said to explain why he was not sleeping in her room. I did not need an explanation. Happiness had returned to my life.

Seeing her breast-feed the baby had a strange effect on me. I noticed that my nipples would get hard when the baby was being fed. Sometimes my breasts became painful, and I could feel wetness on my nipples, as if my breasts were full of milk.

I had difficulty understanding my emotions. Years ago, as a newlywed I remembered being a passionate bride. In recent years I had become manager of a household. Having never become pregnant, I had not encountered the emotions of motherhood. Perhaps it was this new feeling, but something had restarted my dormant biological clock.

One day she had left the baby with me and gone to attend a cousin's engagement party when the feeding time came. I waited for her, but she was late and the boy started crying. I went ahead and let him suck on my nipples. With some effort he was able to get enough to be satisfied and go to sleep by the time she returned.

It became our routine after that. We took turns feeding the baby. It was rather fun and gave me a sense of participation. As usual, people talked and commented. Again, they took it to be saintly on my part. The boy was almost two and was less and less dependent on breast-feeding. I had been feeling queasy every morning and was not sure if something was wrong with the newly harvested wheat which we ate. A couple of times I became dizzy while trying to move a wheat sack across the courtyard.

If I did not know better, I would say that she is pregnant, my husband's aunt commented one day.

It sounded preposterous. I had been married for twenty years and was still childless. Everyone in the extended family understood the division of wifely duties in our house. I was there for managing the household and the second wife was for procreation.

Yes, I who was barren, who was about to be discarded as useless, was now pregnant. I had been restored to my full role in the house. It was summer when I had a baby boy. Our first son was almost three by now. I always loved him more than my own son, and I never forgot the emotions he helped unleash in my body.

The story "The Other Woman" was turned into a film short with the title, Eastern Son, by my nephew Jaffar Mahmood, based on a screen-play prepared by Matthew Okumura. At the last minute, I was also given a bit acting part as a doctor with a 9 second speaking role. What more can a writer ask for?

Long Live the King

Auntie Ji stayed with us past the holiday for the King's birthday. She enjoyed the royal birthday as if it was a carnival. The Fifth King is how she always referred to George V. Strains of Long Live the King had been heard for over two weeks in the village, although what the village band played was barely recognizable as the anthem of the British Empire. The bandmaster only vaguely recalled the tune from his days with the police band.

He is the monarch of the whole Empire, she would tell us. She was fascinated by this far away king who had never set foot in our country.

The new academic year had begun, and the youngest boy in the family, Nikka, was to start school. The men had been busy with the harvest and Nikka's mother, Asho, was busy in the house, and also nervous about dealing with the school bureaucracy.

Auntie Ji was not awed by any of this. She believed in the value of education. I'll take him to school, she said, that way I'll receive blessings as long as he studies well.

On the morning of the first day of school Auntie Ji helped Asho get Nikka ready. The boy

had been scrubbed clean and had bright new clothes on. Auntie Ji showed great enthusiasm in gathering his school supplies and insisted on taking a new reed pen and a wooden writing tablet along.

This is what the child needs to learn words, she said, using paper right away will only ruin his handwriting. She was right, calligraphy is best learned with a reed pen on a wooden tablet smeared with clay. The day before she had been teaching Nikka to wash and prepare the small rectangular wooden board and apply a thin coating of a special clay shale that upon drying made the surface absorbent for calligraphy practice—thus not needing blotting paper or drying powder.

Auntie Ji and little Nikka finally left the house. A little distance away, she stopped and again checked that she had all the essentials to accomplish the school admission, counting aloud.

Birth certificate, calligraphy tablet, sharpened reed pens, tuition money, and you, she said as she pointed to the little boy. She arranged the items—writing tablet under her left arm, money in a pocket sewn on the inside of her dress, birth certificate in the right hand and Nikka in tow holding her left hand. Then she saw the street vendor.

Vendors seem to proliferate around the King's birthday, and this one caught her eye because of the wispy smoke rising from one side of his pushcart. He had a small charcoal stove with a large pot on it. He kept the charcoal at constant heat and the pot at a steady simmer by dropping small dry twigs on the charcoal. As he added each handful of twigs, grey smoke arose, orange tongues of flames lapped around the pot, and the charcoal glowed.

Come here, Auntie Ji, you can't take the little boy to school hungry, said the vendor, who knew her well.

Let me first check to see if you have used honest ingredients.

Only the best for your nephew, only the best.

Nikka looked up at Auntie Ji with wide eyes. Both sat down on low stools that were set up in front of the cart. If cooked right, the mixture of garbanzo beans and sliced potato chunks can be quite delicious. The vendor prepared two plates for them, each plate had a ladle full of beans and potatoes, freshly sliced lime and tomato, a sprinkling of *masala* and cilantro leaves. Here you go, little one. This should help you face the schoolmaster. The vendor handed one plate to Nikka and another to Auntie Ji. She and Nikka had been too busy at home getting prepared, and hadn't eaten anything, and now both dug into the plates of food.

I think your *masala* is too hot for the little boy, Auntie Ji admonished the vendor, finishing her plate. Nikka's eyes were watery, and he was making a steady hissing sound to cool off his burning tongue. The juice vendor was strategically stationed right next to them.

What would you like Auntie Ji? I have orange, pomegranate, and sugar cane juices, he said eagerly. It was only during a brief part of the year he could offer all three.

Sugar cane, of course. Nikka needs to cool off his tongue. It was obvious. Both orange and pomegranate juices, though delicious, are tangy and would have worsened Nikka's condition. The juice vendor fed two pieces of sugar cane into his hand press and started turning the crank. As the flattened stalk emerged at the other side, the glass under the press began filling with juice. He fed in a few pieces of crushed ice that cracked as he turned the crank again, this time with some effort, ensuring that the juice was ice-cold. Auntie Ji watched the little boy with a smile as he took big gulps from his glass. She finished hers and they both walked off.

Auntie Ji, my mouth is still burning, Nikka spoke up as he saw the ice cream vendor— the *kulfi walla.*

She hesitated for a minute and then gave in. All right, but then we must go.

As Auntie Ji and Nikka approached the cart, the vendor gave out his yell again, *Kulfiii.*

What flavor would you like, young one?

Mango.

The vendor could have guessed the answer, this was his best-selling flavor by far. He fished out a steel mold from the crushed ice heap, popped open its top and struck the side of the cart with a swift blow of the mold, loosening the ice-cream popsicle. As it snapped out, he switched hands and handed the popsicle to Nikka, holding the bamboo stick embedded in the frozen milk. Here is your *kulfi*. Nikka began licking gleefully as he walked toward the school.

They had been walking on the path along a small creek for about ten minutes, and as they turned the corner around a farmhouse, they saw the school building on the other side of the creek.

Is that my school, Auntie Ji? The village only had one school, but Nikka's voice had a new sense of pride.

Yes, from now on that is your school. The adobe building had been coated with fresh clay, and the corner room where the headmaster sat had been whitewashed with lime coating. As they approached the small footbridge to cross the creek over to the school side, Nikka became intrigued with a knot of students sitting around a small concrete basin by the side of the creek. Auntie Ji noticed his gaze. They are learning how to wash wool, she said. Nikka had a puzzled look. Yes, wool. It comes from sheep. Auntie Ji smiled. You will also learn this.

It was a good school, and the village was proud of it. When the school was built, along with it came a grant to teach children how to wash and process newly sheared wool. This always fascinated the children, as there were no shepherds living in the village. This was a farming village, and the nomads who raised sheep and visited the village every spring never stayed around long enough to send kids to school. However, year after year the grant money arrived, and teachers dutifully taught the children of farmers how to process wool. No one wanted to inform and embarrass the education department in the capital for fear that the villagers would be considered ingrates. The farm children continued to learn this curious skill they never used in their life.

Auntie Ji and Nikka crossed over the footbridge and entered the school. After some waiting, the headmaster was ready to see them.

So, this is your son—well, come in, bring him over. Do you have everything?

My nephew, and here is his calligraphy tablet. She thrust Nikka and the wooden board at the headmaster.

Well, I don't think he will be needing this right away. Do you have everything else?

Here is the money. She handed it over. He counted it and put it away. She again tried to hand him Nikka. He is all yours, headmaster sahib. Please make him over into anything you wish. We want him to be a success.

The headmaster was being patient, and a number of other parents were waiting. When was he born, do you have any papers?

She started searching for the birth certificate. Under the left arm, in the pocket, in Nikka's pockets—but it was nowhere to be found. She must have put it down on the vendor's pushcart when they stopped for that spicy snack or was it at the juice vendor? No, she thought, it must have been the ice-cream *kulfi walla*. She could go back and find it. The headmaster was beginning to lose patience.

Just tell me when he was born, and you can bring by the papers later.

Her mind was swimming. The boy had to be five years old to enter school, but when was he born? She could recall the morals of many stories, but hard facts seldom stuck in her head.

What is his birthday? The headmaster enquired again.

If I hesitate any longer, she thought, Nikka will not be admitted, he may never go to school—what about his future? She decided to improvise.

The Fifth King, she blurted out.

Pardon me? The headmaster had a puzzled look on his face.

I mean he has the same birthday as the English King, third of June. She was much more confident with fiction, only the facts made her hesitate. Finally, the headmaster understood that she was referring to George the Fifth as The Fifth King.

The vendor had already left, and the birth papers were never found. Auntie told the story of Nikka's admission in a colorful manner and attached much symbolism to the fictional birth date. Another copy of the certificate could

49

have been obtained from the Registrar's office in the city and the records corrected, but Auntie's fabrication was taken as an omen for the child's good luck, and he grew up with a king's birthday.

Garden of the Lunatics
(*Jallianwala Bagh*)

. . . .

*A*untie *Ji* had to mediate a quarrel between two little boys over a loose kite that had floated into the courtyard. They both grabbed it simultaneously. They began struggling over it when she saw and stopped them from tearing it to pieces.

That night she remembered the incident, and her story began with the mention of a kite. Your father, Jumma, was very fond of kites as a child, she said to one of the two who had found the kite earlier in the day.

Little Jumma received a kite as a gift from his uncle who was in town for the Harvest Festival, *Baisakhi*. The little boy rose early to try it out with the first light of day in a small park called *Jallianwala Bagh*, or Garden of the Lunatics. The name of the place may be a distortion of a family's name that once owned this land. It is not much of a garden, or even a very good park, but a plot of dry land as big as two football fields near the city center, surrounded by buildings and approachable only through one very narrow gate. The kite flew beautifully. Young Jumma was satisfied and went home so he could accompany his uncle to the festival.

In the city fairgrounds several miles away, the week-long festival had begun. This had been a good year for crops. People from villages near and far were gathered. They had brought grain, vegetables, and cattle to sell and trade; the fairground was teeming with goats, water buffalos, cows, horses, and donkeys. The animals were paraded at cattle shows and sold at auctions. Thousands of people attended.

The Great War had just ended, and old empires were crumbling in Europe. There was great hope in the land that the British Empire would also fall. The night before there was a political rally at which two prominent leaders, one Muslim and one Hindu, gave speeches asking for freedom. Both were arrested. They were now to be transferred to the military fort across the railroad tracks. Handcuffs had been put on both and a party of twenty or so policemen led them towards the street bridge that crossed the railroad tracks. As they started walking along the street, a small crowd began following the policemen. People were coming out of the alleyways and small cross streets, following the two leaders in a broad spread across the pavement and the sidewalks. The approach to the street bridge was narrow, and the road was getting congested. The policemen kept looking back nervously at the jeering crowd of several hundred. Someone from the crowd threw a rock, and one of the policemen was hit. Several more rocks were thrown, and the policemen panicked. One policeman raised his rifle and opened fire. Two men were hit, the crowd scattered, and policemen walked on with their prisoners to the fort.

Young Jumma and the uncle were at the festival with several other men from our village when they heard the news of this encounter with the police. As the story spread, the mood at the festival turned ugly. An announcement was made in the name of the two leaders that a meeting was being held at the Garden of the Lunatics. The government issued a proclamation. No assembly is permitted. Action will be taken against those found violating the order. The gate to the Garden was locked by the police.

It was early afternoon, and the Harvest Fair was beginning to break up because of the news about the meeting. Many of the villagers had never attended a political rally before and they were excited. The gate to the Garden of the Lunatics was opened forcibly. By late afternoon tens of thousands were jammed in the small park. People drew water from the large well in the center of the park grounds and distributed it to the thirsty. Some speakers arrived and speeches began. Jumma and his uncle were in the crowd.

A group of soldiers arrived, and an officer ordered the crowd to disperse. He told them they were violating the law, but no one paid any attention to him. Fiery, patriotic speeches continued, and the crowd became more and more animated.

Soldiers climbed on top of a nearby building and mounted two machine guns. A final order to disperse was given, but no one left. Soldiers opened fire, and then panic ensued. The uncle shielded Jumma with his own body and got shot in the leg. People were trying to run, they were falling, many were crushed in the melee. Firing continued and there were piles of bodies everywhere in the confined park. It was a massacre of peaceful, unarmed people.

As the evening set in, the soldiers left. Those in the crowd who could walk, began to leave. Jumma accompanied the other men from our village who were able to bandage uncle's leg and carry him home. News traveled like wildfire through the city. Crowds attacked anything that belonged to the Crown. A bank was ransacked. The British bank manager was caught by the crowd. They stood him in the square, poured kerosene over him and set him afire. All the gold and imported cloth stored in the bank was carried away. The bank building was set on fire.

Other Britishers were attacked and five were killed. Some disguised themselves as women in full *burka* and escaped the city. A crowd gathered outside a mission hospital. British nuns who worked as nurses at the hospital were afraid for their lives. Some men from the crowd came to the hospital and made threats against the nurses. The hospital patients, who were not British, got up from their beds in defense of their healers and vowed to protect the nurses. The angry crowd saw this ragtag band of defenders, many in bandages and walking with crutches, and retreated. No one was harmed at the hospital.

In the morning soldiers arrived with reinforcements and order was restored in the city. Leaders who incited others were arrested. Investigations, arrests, summary trials and hangings continued for months. The goods stolen at the bank were traced. The fine imported cloth was especially favored by the villagers and distributed as presents along their return route from the city. Investigations extended to the villages, and anyone with fine imported cloth in his house was arrested.

The uncle's leg finally healed, and he headed back to his village. Throughout his life, the uncle walked with a limp and Jumma never forgot that day in the Garden of the Lunatics—April 13, 1919.

The Debt

Your Uncle Kalam had always been a very methodical man , said Auntie Ji. He learned his work habits as an employee in the government bureaucracy. I am a gazetted officer, he used to say proudly. Checking and overseeing the intricate records of the revenue department, including tax collection, was a complex, bureaucratic job and he had learned to perform it with a flair. Stories of his office encounters with other bureaucrats were legendary, as were tales of his empathy for farmers who faced crop failures or other hardships.

He once borrowed some money from his cousin. It was a short-term loan for a couple of months, and he returned the money with a message to his cousin. Please write a note to me acknowledging the loan return. A couple of weeks later his cousin sent a note on a post card, and some months later forgot all about the whole affair.

Twenty years went by. One day Uncle Kalam and his cousin got into an argument over an inheritance during a family gathering in Uncle's house. The debate became very heated, and right in the middle of it they heard the call for prayer from the mosque across the street. Uncle looked at his watch, and said, Who is this clown calling for prayer. It is too early. He turned to his cousin, Don't go away. Wait here—I will be right back.

He left the house, walking briskly towards the mosque. A couple of minutes later the call for prayer abruptly stopped right in the middle. Soon Uncle Kalam walked in and resumed his argument. As I was saying, you are completely mistaken.

What happened to the *muezzin* (prayer caller)? someone demanded.

I threw him into the ditch. It turned out that Uncle had walked into the mosque, bodily picked up the *muezzin* in the middle of the prayer call, carried him out across the street, and deposited him in a dry irrigation ditch. He was now ready to carry on with the inheritance debate.

His cousin decided to deal a low blow. How can we trust you to be fair in this matter, you have never returned the money you once borrowed from me several years ago. We could see Uncle's forehead beginning to turn purple.

You are mistaken brother. He was trying to remain calm. I did return your money.

No, you did not, his cousin insisted. There were quite a few family members present, and this was a big accusation. There was a hush in the gathering as Uncle left the room. We could hear him rummaging through his bureau in the next room. He returned within five minutes, holding a post card.

Here is the note you sent me twenty years ago. It says here you have received the money. The room fell into dead silence as the cousin stood there, seeming to take forever to finish reading the small postcard.

Yes, he said sheepishly you did return the money. No one questioned Uncle's decisions regarding the inheritance after that.

The Body Thief

*A*untie *Ji* began in a solemn mood. It was late and many of the younger children had already fallen asleep. Tonight's story is about a *Hamzad*. Do you know what a *Hamzad* is?

No, the children answered.

The legend of *Hamzad* is very old. Every human birth is accompanied by the birth of a companion-double, a powerful but invisible being, who can either help or hurt humans. It is probably the same as what the Germans call a *Doppelgänger*. Each one of us has this companion-double whose destiny is bound with ours. At our death, this companion-double is released from the bond and free to go. Some people say you can capture this being at the exact moment of death, especially if it is the death of a young virgin girl. This is the story of one such attempted capture.

Our village had a *mullah* who did not possess much religious knowledge, Auntie Ji continued. What he lacked in knowledge of the doctrines and scriptures, he made up with tales of superstition and black magic. This colorful mix of half-beliefs appealed to the villagers as much as the tales of the prophets and the traditional commandments. The *mullah* had been convincing enough for the farmers and the peasants to keep his job in the village for a number of years. This *mullah* spoke about the legend of *Hamzad* often to Zane, one of the village youth.

Each of us is born with one. When we die, the companion-double, a being made of fire—unlike humans that come from clay—is released. I know how to enslave the *Hamzad*. It can only be done if a young virgin girl dies on the night of the full moon. And if you assist me, we will both possess great powers.

As a handsome young man with land to inherit, Zane was considered by many of the village maidens as the most eligible bachelor. Often, he heard the village girls giggle, and they would steal glances at him as he passed by the well on his way back from the fields. On hot days he would stop and get a drink of freshly drawn water.

Can you help me, Zane? some girl would ask, feigning helplessness in adjusting the wooden pulley that often slipped out of its housing upon his appearance. They watched his flexed muscles and powerful forearms as he rolled up his sleeves and strained to adjust the draw-rope.

On this day, Zane avoided the well and hurried on home. A young girl had died in the village on the eve of the full moon and was already buried. Zane heard the faint wail of the mourners wafting over the breeze, and he shuddered. He was thinking about what the village *mullah* had told him many times.

Zane, if only a young virgin were to die on the night of the full moon, I could show you how to possess great powers.

The sun was setting as Zane entered the house, and his mother called out from the rear courtyard. Is that you, Zane? The *mullah* came by earlier, she said, heightening his anticipation. He greeted her and began to wash up, thinking in the meantime of the girl buried earlier in the day. He had not attended the burial, but the

66

mullah must have officiated and was now eager to carry out his ghoulish scheme.

Zane's mind kept racing through the conversations he and the *mullah* had over the last several months. The *mullah* often amused and regaled the villagers with his fantastical tales, always boasting of his prowess in matters of the unknown. Was the *mullah* serious this time? Did he really intend to go through with what he had said? It did not take long for the *mullah* to show up again—Zane had just finished dinner, and it was getting dark.

Meet me at the cemetery entrance in one hour, the *mullah* whispered, scrutinizing Zane's face. You are not afraid, are you?

Why should I be afraid? Zane snapped back, a little too strongly. Perhaps he was afraid. The *mullah* understood how to manipulate the handsome youth, and this night he needed help. Zane told his mother he was going to visit the village scribe to settle the irrigation water accounts for the season, and not to wait up for him.

It was pitch dark as he left the house and walked south down the macadam road leading out of the congested collection of brick and adobe houses in the village center. Soon he came to the edge of this built-up area. All around the village the houses imperceptibly blended into the fields, but on the south side a large grove of trees from the original forest was left standing. He came upon the grove suddenly and saw the trees looming up ahead. Large bulky shapes of hard wood *Shisham* trees stood in the still night.

He entered the grove and felt a chill as the moon disappeared. He knew the path well, and followed it across the thicket into a clearing, knowing that he was approaching the village cemetery. He could see the low brick wall that marked the original boundary of the graveyard. The wall was beginning to crumble in places, but on the village side it was still considered a strict line of demarcation between the living and the dead. It once circumscribed the whole cemetery, but over the years the cemetery had expanded beyond the wall on the side away from the village.

Zane stood outside the cemetery entrance that was wide enough for four men to carry a coffin through. One wide column on each side of the entrance rose up, topped by a brick archway. He glanced into the cemetery, where he could see that some of the older graves had collapsed, and the dirt had sunk in. Many of the villagers were superstitious about using bricks and mortar for fear of trapping the soul in the ground, so most of the graves were mounds of loose dirt. The moon hung like a Petromax lantern in the cloudless sky. It was two hours to midnight and the only sound piercing the night was an owl in the grove outside the graveyard. The *mullhah* soon showed up, carrying two shovels and a small bundle wrapped in a white towel.

The *Hamzad* can perform miraculous, magical acts, the *mullah* intoned as they prepared to dig. But it must be enslaved properly. The slightest mistake and the whole thing can go wrong. They began shoveling away at the freshly prepared grave of the young girl.

I have knowledge that will help us possess the *Hamzad*. The *mullah* was becoming spirited as they dug deeper. We will both be very rich and possess magical powers. It must have been the stark moonlight and sweat streaking down the *mullah's* flushed face, but he seemed to be frothing at the mouth.

They both kept shoveling and dug down deeper. The dirt in the fresh grave had not yet consolidated; it was loose and porous, and easy to excavate, but the amount was considerable. They kept stabbing down into the earth, scooping up shovelfuls, lifting and throwing away the dirt with a jerky motion.

The loose earth was piling up on the ground to one side of the deepening hole. As the excavation deepened, they had to keep throwing the dirt higher and higher. Zane was doing most of the digging, and the *mullah* was doing much of the huffing and puffing, except when he took breaks to talk.

I have spent many years of my life preparing for this night. I know the exact techniques for taking control of the powerful entity. This night will completely change our lives.

Zane kept digging quietly. It was obvious the *mullah* could not have accomplished the sheer

physical task of digging a six foot long and four-foot-wide hole, down six feet. Zane was now unsure why he had agreed to the whole thing, but he felt challenged and was not about to back out.

By now, the cavity in the ground had been cleaned of loose earth, and their shovels were hitting the hard soil. They were both standing at the base of the grave, with only Zane's head above the adjacent ground surface. The grave had been prepared in the Punjabi fashion; a rectangular hole six feet straight down with a side niche at the base for the body. Direct moonlight illuminated a portion of the grave's bottom, as a sharp diagonal line defined the boundary between light and shadow. Zane squatted down and fumbled with his hands looking for the burial niche. Flat sun-dried bricks covering the niche had been set with clay mortar that was still moist. Upon feeling the damp earth, Zane used the tip of the shovel to pry open one of the bricks, after which the *mullah* also joined in. Soon they had removed all the bricks and opened up the burial niche in the side of the grave. The girl's body was shrouded in layers of white cloth with extra lengths of fabric around her head and feet. Kneeling in the base of the grave, they reached into the niche, each grabbed one end of the cloth shroud, and with some effort pulled the limp form out.

With a lift from Zane, the *mullah* climbed out of the grave. After catching his breath, he sat down at the edge of the excavation, and as Zane lifted the shrouded corpse up, the *mullah* grabbed hold of it, pulling it out of the grave. Zane climbed out and they both half lifted and half dragged the girl's body, still wrapped in the white cloth, away from the grave. Zane was now sure he had made a mistake, and mentally counted how many different commandments, rules of conduct, and tenets of decency he had already violated. He began thinking he should just leave but the *mullah* kept him enmeshed in his web of mystery, bravado and greed with continuous exhortations and challenges.

Zane sat down to rest, leaning against a tree trunk, and watched the *mullah* mumble incantations as he unwrapped the white shroud. Now the *mullah's* attention was wholly on the corpse, while Zane's horror and loathing rose higher and became more intense. Within a few minutes the girl's nude body was stretched out on the white cloth laid upon the ground. Every fiber in Zane's body was taut as he looked at the girl's face; her pallor was deepened in the moonlight, heightened by her long black hair. He shuddered. He had seen the girl many times at the well.

The *mullah* began a new chant in a deeper cadence with an altered voice as he drew a circle on the ground around the corpse. He spread her arms and legs outward as her lifeless form lay face up. He then unfurled the white towel he had brought, took out four large straight knives, and stuck them in the ground outside the circle, one knife each near her hands and feet. The knives glistened in the moonlight. He then motioned to Zane to get up. The *mullah* made him stand near her feet, outside the circle, facing her body.

He himself stood near the head of the girl and began a vehement, steady chant made up of words and sounds completely unintelligible to Zane, though he thought he heard the girl's name mentioned a number of times and his own once. Zane stole a glance at her still face, could not bear it, and looked away. His eyes glided across the moonlit terrain, and he fixed his gaze at the grove of trees twenty yards off.

It seemed to Zane that the incantations continued for a long time, although perhaps less than an hour had elapsed. Zane kept his eyes affixed on the trees as much as he could, casting occasional glances at the *mullah* who was mumbling with his eyes closed as if in a trance. All the while the girl's lifeless form lay motionless on the ground, faintly glistening in the moonlit night.

Over an hour had gone by when Zane, from the corner of his eye, noticed a slight movement in her body, as if a shudder went through it. He looked down, did not detect any change, and then saw it happen—the girl shuddered again as if some otherworldly energy had touched her. The *mullah's* chant had slowed to a hypnotic drone and Zane recalled their earlier conversation. The

Hamzad wants to occupy the body. He imagined the ghostly *Hamzad* hovering around the circle, eager to enter the body and possess it. The shudders in the corpse were now more frequent and soon changed into slow convulsive movements, as if a struggle was going on—the *Hamzad* trying to possess the body and the *mullah* trying to attain control over the *Hamzad*.

The convulsions suddenly quieted down, and the body movements became more deliberate. The *Hamzad* appeared to have entered the body and was struggling to get out of the surrounding circle. The outstretched arms were groping for something, and Zane saw one of the hands push its way out of the circle and reach for a knife.

Zane had been overcome with fear ever since the body movements began. He suddenly bolted, running for his life, and making a mad dash for the grove of trees. As he entered the grove, and ran around a large tree trunk, he heard the whoosh of an object flying through the air, and the twangy thud of a metallic item piercing the tree. He stole a glance and saw one of the long straight knives embedded in the tree trunk. The *Hamzad*, using the girl's body had thrown the knife after him. It was then that it dawned on Zane—he had been brought there as a human sacrifice for the newly freed *Hamzad*, somehow a necessary part of the conjuration. He kept running, leaving the *mullah* to battle it out with the ghostly demon, and did not stop until he reached home and went to bed.

Zane slept fretfully. Something had gone wrong last night. He was going to see the *mullah* to find out how he had fared. He left the house and saw a small group of men on the street corner, huddled around the grave digger who was talking excitedly. Yes, I swear I am telling the truth. I went this morning to the cemetery to prepare the grave for a headstone. The grave had been dug up, and the dead *mullah* was stretched out on the ground. Three knives had pierced his chest, and the girl's body lay on top of him—naked as the day she was born.

Zane stole back home, feeling nauseated, and sat all day on his cot, unable to go to the farm. It took a long time for his nightmares to stop and even longer for things to sort out in his head. The *mullah* obviously took him along as a human sacrifice for the newly awakened *Hamzad*, but when he escaped, the *mullah* became the sacrifice. Because two shovels were found by the grave, many people suspected that a second person was helping the *mullah*, but no one knew who it was.

Twenty years went by, and most people in the village forgot the whole ghoulish affair. It was then that Zane recounted his involvement to a couple of close friends, one of whom was from our family.

Lord Mountbatten

Auntie Ji had been visiting us for about a week. It was after dinner on a midwinter evening, and all the kids were crowded around a pot-belly stove. Some of us were munching on pocketfuls of shelled almonds and raisins. One of the boys placed a thick, juicy raisin on the hot stove; the raisin swelled up, began sizzling, and then splattered. The boy burst into laughter, immediately drawing Auntie Ji's wrath.

No story tonight if you do that again. The miscreant snickered sheepishly and drew back.

Others spoke up in unison, as if to neutralize this naughty act.

Story, Auntie Ji—please tell us a story.

Auntie Ji began.

It was a cold winter evening like tonight, and our family was going for your Uncle Namdi's wedding. About twenty of us from the groom's family were to travel together and had to board a train. We had prepared several suitcases full of gifts for the bride's family, including clothing and jewelry. The groom was dressed in distinctive clothing, and our group was easily identifiable as a wedding party.

Four *tonga* horse drawn carriages had been hired to take us to the railway station, and the suitcases were loaded up along with the passengers. As we neared the railroad station, we found the main approach road full of policemen. It turned out that Lord Mountbatten was leaving on a train, and an honor guard was seeing him off. We had to get off our carriages and make our way to the station on foot. It was very crowded, and we were afraid we were going to miss our train.

The prospect of delay threw the groom's father into a panic. He was a former military officer and decided to take command of the situation.

Turn this way. Stop here. Unload these suitcases. Wait for me, don't move, he barked orders to the *tonga wallas*, porters and guests alike, and was making everyone feel tense. He was also carrying everyone's train tickets for safekeeping in his inside jacket pocket. One of the cousins said under his breath, It seems Lord

Mountbatten hasn't left; he is right here with us. Everyone laughed, and the tension eased a bit. The nickname stuck to the groom's father.

We proceeded on to the station accompanied by a line of porters. The station was packed with people coming and going. Villagers with bundles on their heads, vendors hawking their goods and food sellers were all competing for space. It took a lot of effort to keep everyone together. Being an easily recognizable wedding party, we were also a target for pickpockets.

We managed to cross the maelstrom and find our train carriage. After some delay the train left the station, and about half an hour later a ticket checker walked into our compartment. We pointed to the groom's father, who searched one pocket, then a second one, and a third. The tickets were nowhere, nor was his wallet. His pockets had been picked clean. We had to pay for the tickets again, plus a penalty. No one was laughing this time and there was an edge to it when someone hissed, Lord Mountbatten.

When we arrived at the bride's family compound, they had prepared one of the houses for our stay. The front room's door opened onto the street, and the men in our party were relaxing there. A stranger walking by in the alley stopped, looked at our wedding party, and entered with a greeting. He was a tall man with a fair complexion and a handlebar mustache that gave him a stately look. He was well-dressed and spoke with an authoritative voice, I happened to be passing by and saw you all gathered here. I am new to this town. What occasion brings you all together?

Some men felt it was intrusive of this man but were unsure how to deal with the stranger. Our Mountbatten decided to take charge again and deal with him as an equal. The stranger kept asking probing questions about our family's background, and the conversation turned testy. Mountbatten spoke forthrightly, demonstrating that we had nothing to hide. After a while the two were almost friendly. The incident about the pickpockets was mentioned and laughed about. Though his identity remained unclear, the stranger's departure was almost cordial.

The wedding reception was held in the evening, and we were surprised to see the tall stranger at the reception. He turned out to be the bride's uncle from out of town. He had been opposed to this union and did not want to agree until he had investigated and checked our family background anonymously on his own. He laughingly revealed his earlier conversation with us to all the guests. The only adverse information I learnt is this family is an easy target for pickpockets. Even Lord Mountbatten cannot protect them. Everyone laughed and the wedding ceremonies went on smoothly. The groom's father became known as Lord Mountbatten to the bride's family too.

A Prisoner of War

. . . .

O*ne night,* Auntie Ji began very seriously. This is a story about your Uncle Malik. He used to work as a policeman in Hong Kong and was taken prisoner by the Japanese during the Second Great War. In the prison camp the Japanese guards put him on kitchen duty, and this is what happened one day.

As always, Malik was given lentils and rice that were full of grit, which was going to take him all day to sift before he could cook dinner for his barracks. The Japanese guards were standing dutifully in the kitchen and by the gate in the fence. The other prisoners were doing hard labor at the bridge construction site. They were going to return in the evening, expecting food to be ready, dinner being their only meal of the day.

Malik worked on the rice first, spreading a little bit of it on a flat slate in front of the barracks, and picking out little grey and tan colored rocks. He moved handfuls of rice around, spread them so he could spot the small rocks and push them to one side of the large slate. He then repeated the same process with lentils, finding it harder to pick out the grit among the yellow lentils.

He had never been sure if the Japanese soldiers intentionally mixed the dirt and rocks in, or if the grain had been contaminated during open storage on some unpaved warehouse floor. It had to be the lowest quality food he had ever tasted, and there wasn't much of it. He longed for the freshly harvested wheat and the lentils of his native village in Punjab.

Malik had the rice and lentils sifted by late afternoon and needed to go to the back of the barracks to pick up firewood.

Halt, the Japanese guard barked at him and picked up his rifle. Malik pointed to the back of the building and stood at attention waiting. The guard waved him and put the rifle down.

This was routine. The guard knew where Malik was going, but he did manage to scare him each time. Once behind the barracks, Malik quickly climbed up onto the thatched roof and began picking some weeds he had planted there. The guards either did not know about it or didn't care, but the greens provided the only fresh vegetables in the prisoners' diet.

The sun was about to set when the prisoners on work detail returned. Malik's barrack-mates ate their meager rations, slumped down on their straw mats and were soon asleep.

This camp was in eastern Burma, and held Burmese, Indian, and Chinese prisoners—all from the British army. Malik had been a police-man in Hong Kong, trying to keep peace, not fight a war. Perhaps the Japanese prison guards understood the distinction between Malik and the soldier prisoners, or maybe it was his friendly manner. In any case, they usually assigned him light duties.

The next morning's assembly was before sunrise and all of the two hundred or so prisoners were lined up. The prisoners from each barrack had little contact with those from another barrack. A couple of new Japanese officers were standing by the flag. They must have arrived during the night with the latest news from the front, and perhaps some new orders.

Prisoners, the camp commander howled, today ten of you are going to be transferred to another camp for early release. A muffled cheer went up through the ragtag assembly.

Also, he continued, the official investigation has been completed, and collaborators have been identified. Therefore, ten of you will be executed.

A hush fell over the prisoners. Rumors of the investigation had been circulating for weeks. It was focused on resistance activities that took place during the early period of Japanese occupation. The Japanese had been frustrated at the inability to root out the resistance leaders.

Here are the first ten names, one of the lieutenants said. As he read each name, a prisoner stepped forward, and soon all ten were standing together.

Tools were distributed to the prisoners, and they were ordered to pick up shovels and pickaxes. Two guards stepped up and began escorting the men out of the camp. As they were leaving the camp, the other group of ten was being assembled. One of the guards ordered

Malik to come along. About a mile or so from the camp, they stopped, and one of the guards told the prisoners to start digging a trench. Although they were often told to do seemingly meaningless tasks just as punishment, this trench seemed particularly useless. It did not connect with any ditch or water course.

The trench was almost completed when one of the prisoners came up to a guard and asked, What are we doing?

The guard looked at him indignantly, paused for a moment and said, Why, you are digging you own grave.

The prisoner's face drained, What do you mean. I am to be released today. Look at your list.

The guard muttered but took out his list. He read out the names. It was no use—the prisoner's name was on the list. The prisoner was puzzled and said, Look on the other list, the release list. The guard was getting annoyed. He flipped the page and looked at the other list.

Yes, the same name is on this list also. Apparently, there were two prisoners in the camp with the same name. Others also stopped digging and everyone looked at the guard. Malik was standing behind him.

I am innocent. I was never part of the resistance. When the lieutenant started calling the names, I assumed we were going to be released, so I stepped forward. The prisoner was desperate.

The guard spoke with the other guard, thought for a moment, then turned to the petitioner, Look, the other group left soon after we left, and they are long gone by now. If I take you back, there will be questions. This is all your stupidity. You are going to die one day anyway.

The prisoners were told to stand along the trench and bow their heads. One guard gave a swift blow with a sword to the back of the neck, the other kicked from the back and the body fell into the trench.

All ten were executed this way. Malik was ordered to backfill the trench and carry the tools back to the camp. He had many stories from the war years, but this stayed with him the longest.

The Farmer's Snack

. . . .

T̶onight, said Auntie Ji, I'll tell you an incident from a long time ago when your grandfather Mahi was still living in the village and farming the ancestral land.

One day Mahi came back from the field very tired and hungry. October was the busiest month of the year, when he had to plow the largest parcel in preparation for sowing wheat. Three sharecroppers lived on his land, helped him with the farm chores and received a share of the crop. Of the three, one had been sick, so Mahi had to do the job of two men.

I am hungry, he yelled as he entered the family compound.

Come on in, said his wife, Kamo. I am making your favorite snack, and dinner will be ready in a little while. She had kneaded a large pan of wheat dough for the whole family. A tray full of raw sugar was next to it and a deep *karahi* wok of *ghee* was on the

94

stove. Mahi sat down on a low hemp stool near her in the kitchen.

She rolled and flattened a pat of dough, filled it with raw brown sugar, folded and tucked its edges into a *samosa-like* shape and dropped it into sizzling *ghee*. As it fried to a crisp brown, she rolled additional patties, and then took the cooked fritter out of the *ghee* and offered it to Mahi.

This is delicious, he exclaimed, breaking off another piece and putting it in his mouth. He liked these sweet *empanada-like* fritters and could usually eat three or four at a sitting.

A sweet aroma was spreading in the kitchen. The sweet, rich dough fritters were turning a deep brown with a crisp crust and a soft interior. Three, sometimes four pieces were frying at the same time. As each came to a light brown, she took it out and placed it on a palm frond basket-woven tray in front of him. As soon as the excess *ghee* was absorbed, he picked it up and bit into it.

He ate the usual fourth piece, but then did not stop—he kept on eating.

You are going to ruin your appetite, Kamo said, when Mahi was on his seventh or eighth piece. He still did not stop, and her attention stayed on the frying wok with sizzling *ghee*.

It is going to be a good and plentiful crop this year, Mahi said. The ground is perfect, and the sowing has been going well. The new fertilizer blends very smoothly, and I can sense the fertility in the earth. He was in an ebullient mood, and kept on talking, as if to himself. Kamo had made the dough for the whole family. The mound of dough was getting smaller, yet there were no fried fritters in the tray. She thought of reminding him again but did not want to disrupt his happy chatter and kept quiet. After all he has been working doubly hard to get the planting done before the winter rains come. He must be on his twelfth piece by now.

I think I am going to buy another horse after the harvest. There are days when I just cannot get my errands done on time, he said as he picked up another fritter. His eating kept pace with her frying.

I am feeling better now. Is the next one ready? he asked as he swallowed the last mouthful for the 25th dough roll.

After a little while longer, she came to the end of the dough. He looked a little surprised.

Is it all finished?

Yes, you have eaten all 32 pieces that I was making for the whole family. And the dinner will be ready soon. He looked puzzled as he tried to get up from the low stool, staggered and sank back. He had a helpless look on his face.

I cannot get up, he moaned, holding his stomach.

Just keep sitting. Let them all settle down, she said to soothe him.

After some time, he was able to stand up. He staggered outside and walked back to the fields he had been planting. He picked up a large log usually pulled by a bull to break up the clods in the freshly plowed field. He put the log on his shoulder and started walking toward the irrigation canal about one mile away. He walked back and forth ten times before his stomach settled some so he could breathe easily and sit down without an ache in his belly. He ate no dinner that night and never quite relished the dough-rolled fritters again.

The Real Bride

*A*untie *Ji* had gone to visit some relatives in the next neighborhood and was expected back in the evening. All the children had been told to keep their eyes open, considering how often she got lost in our neighborhood. In an open field just beyond our neighborhood, one of the boys who was almost eight had been trying to learn to ride a bicycle for many days, and to his astonishment he was finally able to do it. It was an exhilarating feeling. The air rushed past his flushed cheeks and tickled his hair. He first rode straight ahead, pedaling as hard as he could. Then he made a long, winding curve and marveled at how he could bank the bike. He kept going into tighter and tighter circles while pedaling harder, until some pebbles under the tire almost threw him into a skid. He recovered and got off the bike for the day.

It was a full-size bike that belonged to his father. He was away on business out of town, and the boy had been sneaking the bike out of the house, walking it to the playground and learning how to ride. He couldn't reach the pedals if he sat up on the saddle, so he had been riding the bike scissors-style, putting one leg through the frame, and had finally mastered the odd balancing act. He decided to ride the bike all the way home—wanting his friends in the neighboring houses to see him.

The hissing of bike tires on firm ground was hypnotic. The odd acrobatic style of riding, once mastered, felt smooth, though rather strenuous, but he could feel how each push of the pedal accelerated the wheels. He had to concentrate on the complex task of balancing by leaning the bike to one side, while leaning his own body in the opposite direction at just the appropriate angle. He was approaching his alley, and just as he started to make the turn he was distracted by chants of Auntie, Auntie.

He looked away from the bike to try and locate where Auntie was and saw some kids running in her direction. Just then he felt the wheels give way as he spotted a vendor sitting on the street corner. The banking angle he had worked out in the playground could not be maintained, and as the wheels skidded, he careened into the vendor, scattering his wares all over. The vendor fell off his stool amid popcorn, sand-roasted grains, and the sesame-coated white sugar candy. Auntie Ji was close enough to witness the whole thing. She quickened her step to rescue the boy.

Auntie Ji you saw the whole thing, this boy is totally reckless. The vendor was trying to get a negotiating advantage.

Yes, yes, I saw it. It is not his fault, it was an accident, she said, defending her nephew. She put down her armload of presents she had brought for everyone, took out a wallet from a pocket sewn in her dress, and handed the vendor eight *Anas*.

Here, she said, this is twice what your stuff was worth. Go and get new supplies. The vendor gathered his baskets and walked away muttering. The boy hugged Auntie Ji and then sheepishly walked the bike behind her.

As they entered the house, the boy's mother greeted Auntie and got the news from her.

Congratulations, sister. Your son just got a lesson in bike riding, and I paid his tuition. Both laughed and by late evening the incident was forgotten.

After dinner all the children gathered around Auntie. Story, Auntie Ji, please tell us a story. A treasure-house of family lore, she probably told these stories to keep the family traditions alive, but the children enjoyed them anyway. She addressed one of the cousins.

I'll tell you about how your grandmother became part of our family. Your grandfather was a handsome young man and was making a good living with his farm and his horse ranch. Our family had received several proposals from good families with pretty girls of marriageable age.

But, Auntie Ji, isn't that shameful? One of the teenage girls already knew that upstanding families with pretty girls received proposals; they didn't send them.

What can you say? It was right after the war, and there weren't many young men around who still had all four limbs intact.

Anyway, after a lot of discussions and advice from different people, our family decided on a girl. Her name was Neelam. She had fair skin, embroidered and cooked very well, and prayed regularly. Everyone said good things about her.

Well, then, did they get married? One of the children was impatient.

Be patient and listen. Just as things were being firmed up, we started getting pressure from a rich family in town. They had somehow assumed their daughter had the right to marry the most eligible bachelor.

After some more debate we finally relented, and preparations began for the marriage with the rich girl. Once we agreed and announced the engagement publicly, the girl's family started making all kinds of demands. They wanted the 24-carat gold jewelry to be made in a lace design. And the dresses had to be made with imported fabrics. They were being quite unreasonable.

But why did we put up with that? asked one of the older boys.

Son, between the engagement and marriage is a very critical period. Both families must deal with the other very delicately. Finally, the wedding day arrived. The wedding party had arranged for a number of horse-drawn carriages, and that is how all the guests rode to the bride's house five miles away—in carriages.

That must have been fun, mused one boy, A long procession of carriages.

And all the women in bright new shiny clothes, one of the girls added.

Yes, it was grand. Trunks full of presents were loaded up in the carriages along with the guests and all the right jewelry that had been prepared. Upon arrival at the bride's house, our family got out and the carriages waited to take us back. We sat down and were served with the traditional milk and rose water cold drinks. Then they started to draw up the wedding papers. Our family had taken our own scribe along just to be sure. After taking a look at the papers, our scribe whispered to your grandfather that the contract amount was totally out of line with our family traditions.

What is this cataract mound? a small boy asked sheepishly. The other children laughed.

Auntie was patient.

At the time of a wedding, some papers are written up showing the name of the bride and the groom and mentioning a sum of money. If the groom ever wants to divorce the bride, he must pay up that amount to the bride. Our family has always believed that marriages last because of trust, not because the money is too much for the groom to pay, so we don't believe the amount should be very large. Your grandfather explained this very respectfully to the bride's father.

Sir, he said, five thousand rupees is inappropriate. Our tradition dictates that we limit this amount to two rupees. I give you my word that my son will treat your daughter with respect. A large amount only leads to ill feelings.

The girl's family felt they were being insulted by suggesting a low amount. Your grandfather was furious.

If you want to put a price on your daughter, I'll go home right now, get five thousand rupees, and pay you in cash. But we are not going to go against our tradition and include this in the marriage papers.

The arguments became louder. Finally, your grandfather said, Let us go. The wedding party got up, walked out of the house, and started getting into the waiting carriages. No one could believe what was happening.

As the carriages left the bride's house, everyone was feeling downcast. Your grandfather was in the first carriage, directing the coachman, and we noticed the procession was not heading home. He had ordered the first carriage to proceed to Neelam's house, the pretty and talented girl we had originally chosen. When we arrived there, some makeshift arrangements were already being made to receive the wedding party. He had sent them an advanced messenger, but they had only a few minutes before the guests arrived. It took several hours. Dinner was cooked, the bride dressed up, and the contract papers drawn. The bride's family was bewildered but happy. And that is how your grandmother became part of the family. She ended up being the real bride of that day.

Opium Baby

*A*untie *Ji* was often oblivious to the reality around her—lost in her thoughts, or in an imaginary world of fantasy. Many tales were told of her absent-mindedness.

Coming to see us, she walked from her village for about three miles to get to the main road. From there she caught a ride in a *tonga* horse carriage to the main market in the city five miles away, and then walked another mile to get to our house. It was early spring, and as she got off the carriage near the market, she saw a sugar cane vendor. He had peeled and cut up the juicy, sweet sugarcane into foot-long pieces. She knew how much the kids would like the fresh sugar cane, so she bought some. Her hands were already full of candy and the small hand-crafted toys she had brought from the village, so she put the small tied-up bundle of foot-long sugar cane pieces under her left arm.

After walking a mile, she was approaching our alley when she decided to check and make sure she had everything with her. Yes, she still had the toys and candy from the village and had not forgotten anything in the carriage. But what about the sugar cane? She looked at the items in her right hand, and then in the left, but could not see the sugar cane. I must have forgotten it where I bought it, she thought. She walked all the way back to the market and found the vendor still there.

Excuse me, I bought some sugar cane from you, but I forgot it in your cart. Do you still have my bundle?

The vendor smiled, Sister, what is your name?

What do you want with my name? She was irritated, Tell me if you have seen my sugar cane that I paid for.

Please tell me your name, and then I will answer your question, he said, still smiling.

My name is Bholi. Auntie's name literally meant Innocent Maiden.

The vendor laughed out loud, angering Auntie even more. Dear Innocent Maiden, what is that tucked under your arm? She looked,

111

thanked him, and walked away. Nothing fazed her.

As a teenager she had a reputation for a lot of spunk. Her mother had died quite young, and when Auntie Bholi was a teenager, her father remarried. Soon after the second marriage, another daughter was born.

One day the teenage Bholi spanked her younger stepsister for some naughtiness. The child complained to her mother, who scolded Bholi. When the father came home in the evening, his new wife complained to him, and he also decided to discipline Bholi. She was busy with some chores in the yard when he called her angrily.

Bholi!

Yes, father, what is it? She looked up to see him walking briskly toward her, and stopped what she was doing.

Did you hit your sister today? His tone was very sharp.

The teenage Bholi stood up to her full height, very erect, with a hurt but defiant look on her face, and stared coldly at her father. After a pause she said, You too, father? The mother is already on her side. He was taken aback and stood there quietly. She looked him straight in the eye, I was wondering why you were coming toward me like a charging bull. She never had any trouble with her father or her stepmother after that day.

We always thought she was wonderful. She brought us presents, told us stories, and taught us simple games from the village. I had always wondered how she turned from a plucky teenager into a forgetful and loving adult. It was many years later when I learned the following events.

Soon after her marriage Auntie Bholi was blessed with a daughter of her own—a beautiful, healthy, plump and good-natured baby who often laughed. Auntie loved the girl, and wherever she went, took the baby along. During one of her three-mile walks to the next village, she was carrying the baby, and felt very tired, but being in a hurry, could not stop to rest. She saw a small shrine along the way, and as she was walking by, picked up a straw from the ground, and facing the shrine, said, If you are a true saint, please make this baby as thin as this straw. Then she won't be this heavy.

We don't know if any person, let alone a saint is buried in that shrine. But soon afterward, the girl began losing weight. Within six months she was reduced to a skeletal figure of skin and bones. Somehow the balance of nutrients in her body had been upset, and she became malnourished. The happy, healthy baby became transformed into a moaning, fretting, crying mass of bones that was always clinging to her mother. The baby's face was hideous to look at, and others rarely offered to hold her.

Why did I have to say those words; I did not want my baby to suffer. Auntie often blamed herself for having begged the ominous supplication of the saint, but no one saw Auntie cry or sulk. She still managed to visit people and participate in family gatherings without any complaint.

While at home in the village, Auntie still had her chores to do. Opium could be purchased at government stores in small quantities for medicinal purposes. It was not unusual that if an infant was teething or sick, and could not sleep, mothers would put a tiny speck of opium on the baby's tongue as a pacifier. If a sickly little baby was given a tiny amount of opium, it could rest and sleep for three to four hours, giving the mother an opportunity to complete her household chores.

Auntie started to buy a small amount for her little girl who was always moaning, crying, and clinging to her. This seemed to be the only way for the baby to rest and for Auntie to finish her chores. The opium store would sell her a small amount in a paste form wrapped in wax paper, which would last for a few weeks.

Auntie came to visit us in the city for the Eid festival. We were expecting many guests, and the whole household was busy with preparations. Auntie had always guided us in preparing the vermicelli dessert, and she wanted to help on this day also. She brought the opium along with the baby, but it had almost run out, and the wax paper looked clean. The baby was fidgety the previous night and had also not been able to keep any food down. Auntie rinsed the wax

115

paper and fed the water to the baby, who fell asleep. Auntie helped out in the kitchen, and when the vermicelli dish was ready, she changed into new clothes to welcome the guests.

She went to pick up the sleeping girl, and with the child in her lap, participated in all festivities. Everyone was used to seeing the sick baby in Auntie's lap. The guests had arrived, and a big roaring feast was held, including presents for all the children and new clothes for the adults.

Just as the guests left, Auntie spoke, I don't know why this child does not move. When a couple of the adults checked, the girl had been dead for several hours, and her body was cold. It was the baby's long illness, or the overdose of opium, or both. Auntie probably knew the baby was dead but did not want the festivities ruined with a sad incident, so she spent the whole day with the motionless child in her lap, ignoring reality. Some people say she was never the same after that, and often could not tell fantasy or her daydreams apart from reality.

The Land Settlement

*T*he *children* were all gathered in the courtyard awaiting the nightly story from Auntie Ji. One of the younger boys kept teasing his older sister. Her hair was braided with colorful ribbons and tiny bells. He tugged at it to make the bells jingle a few times until finally she screamed at him. Auntie Ji pulled the boy over and sat him down close to her.

This is the story of how your great grandfather, Ameer, came into his land. The last Mogul Emperor had died, she began. The news came to the village, as all other important news arrived, through the *chowkidar*, the village watchman. He had gone to the city to collect his monthly salary, register the deaths and births in the village during the past month, and to bring back all current news. No one in the village had ever seen the emperor. He lived in the far away capital, and over the last few years he was not even the actual ruler of

the country. He had been imprisoned by the British and had died in prison. But all the villagers felt their great protector had left them. The British Crown began implementing the final steps in their occupation of India.

Rumors of impending upheavals began circulating. Ameer's uncle, Alam, was the clearinghouse for political rumors in the village. He had lost a leg in the 1857 uprising that the British referred to as The

Mutiny, but being on the losing side did not even receive the customary pension for wounded veterans.

Mutiny? Alam would holler whenever he heard the word. It was our War for Independence, and if more of you had joined, we would have been successful. He had become Uncle for the whole village, and as such regularly held his evening assembly to dispense wit and commentary as the resident sage.

We should have thrown the *Farangi* into the ocean, right where he came from, and let him swim back to his cold island. Our village was far from the ocean, and most of the villagers had never seen the sea, so the tales of naval prowess mystified us.

But Uncle, what for? Our king's dynasty would have ended anyway, one of them teased him. The emperor had not produced an heir brave enough to take back the throne—a sensitive and sore point with all those who had participated in the uprising. No one dared question the emperor's manhood in Uncle's presence, but in Uncle's absence many jokes were told about the king's many wives and the palace eunuchs. Was he one of them?

Yes, yes, I know very well what you traitors and cowards are hinting at. Maybe it was written then, for the Empire to come to this end. The conversation turned to what changes the British would implement in the village.

Ameer was nearly sixteen, just old enough to be accepted in these evening gatherings, but he kept his mouth shut. That night, the conversation had turned to rumors of impending land assessment and the topic interested him intensely. This rumor had been brought by the village watchman, but he and everyone else were having trouble grasping the concept of land ownership. There seemed to be unlimited land in every direction around the village, and each family farmed as big a parcel as they could manage. Larger families had more mouths to feed and farmed larger parcels, while the smaller families needed and farmed less—all they could feasibly manage.

But Uncle, how can they stop us from adding land to our fields? Look at Ameer, he will soon be claiming his share.

They were talking about the age-old custom of our village. For as long as anyone could remember, our village had had this custom. As each male turned sixteen, he had the right to go out and claim his land for cultivation and ownership. People would turn out to watch him stake his claim. Ameer had been preparing to make his claim by practicing with two oxen and a plow, which by now he could handle very well. On the day of the spring festival in his sixteenth year, he was to go beyond the last cultivated field and mark his own plot of land, comprising all that he could circumscribe using his plow between sunrise and sunset. Ameer had been scouting and had an area in mind.

But how, asked the village watchman defiantly, how can they prevent us from plowing more? Are they going to put the land in their pocket and carry it away? He looked around but no one said anything. They were all equally confounded by the concept of ownership of farmland. Well, are they? he repeated.

Everyone seemed impressed by this argument. We could see the logic. Inside a village or a city, one can own land by building on it, but out in the fields and farms, with no fences or walls, how would land be marked? One cannot carry it around, so how can it be owned? You can own money, clothes, gold, and even wheat and corn, because you can carry these things with you. But land can only be cultivated, lived on, and traveled across. You are born on it, die on it, and can choose to be buried in it. But if you are not a dweller or a cultivator, and the land is not being used by anyone for any other purpose, how can you prevent others from using it? And especially how can it be owned or restricted by a faraway Raj? Uncle looked pensive and patient, as if he was dealing with children.

They have been waiting for the emperor to die. This new land assessment is going to change everything. No one seemed impressed with this line of thinking. After all, he was not really refuting the *chowkidar's* logic. The villagers seemed to have convinced themselves they were always going to have access to all the land they wanted to cultivate or build on.

A few days later Uncle suggested that Ameer should go through with his land demarcation ceremony and not wait for the spring festival. Some in the village frowned upon it at first, but eventually acquiesced to moving up Ameer's ceremony. Ameer was happy, and proceeded to perform the ceremony, setting a sizable claim. Soon afterward Uncle's reasoning became clear to everyone.

A party of surveyors and one scribe arrived from the city, accompanied by two policemen with rifles. They had orders in hand to implement the land assessment. They proceeded to measure and record plans, and write down what and how much land each family had been cultivating and issued title papers with names and property boundaries. They posted signs on the land beyond the cultivated fields. Everything became fixed in time for the villagers after that. Ameer, your great grandfather, was the last young man to claim new land in our old customary manner.

Acknowledgements

My late wife *Maliha Mendoza Mahmood* designed, typed, and helped me publish the text-only First Edition of *The Village Clock* in 1999.

Martha Fuller and Sharon Rawlins created a complete re-design for this new illustrated Second Edition 2023, which now includes artwork by my daughter AliA. Martha guided me in smoothing out the previous text and Sharon melded the text with AliA's paintings into this charming collection.

About the Author

Arshud Mahmood was born in India, grew up in Pakistan, and came to California over 50 years ago. He received a Ph.D. in engineering from the University of California, Berkeley and works as a consulting engineer. The ancient Indus Valley Civilization is an area of personal interest and study for him—harking back to his Punjabi family. His curiosity about this ancient civilization is expressed in his imaginative novel—*Dancing Girl of the Indus Valley* (2023) available on Amazon and Barnes & Noble—paperback or eBook. His first short collection, *Coffee with Chicory: And Other Stories of Cultural Crossroads* (2011) is also available on Amazon and Barnes & Noble—paperback or eBook. This new collection of illustrated folk tales *The Village Clock* is an updated illustrated Second Edition of a 1999 text-only version.

About the Illustrator

AliA was born in California, spent her childhood in Texas and Alaska, and currently lives in Southern California. She received a B. A. in Fine Art from Art Center College of Design in Pasadena and works as a freelance artist—creating paintings, drawings, tattoos, and wearable art.
(aliatalent@gmail.com)

This book is typeset in Museo, a contemporary semi-serif typeface. Display type is Reiner Script and is used on the cover along with Orpheus Pro, a serif typeface.

Milton Keynes UK
Ingram Content Group UK Ltd.
UKHW020842301123
433406UK00012B/152